FRANCHISING IN ETHIOPIA 2014

Legal and Business Considerations

KENDAL H. TYRE, JR., EXECUTIVE EDITOR
DIANA VILMENAY-HAMMOND, MANAGING EDITOR
COURTNEY L. LINDSAY, II, ASSISTANT EDITOR

LexNoir Foundation

First Quarter 2014

LexNoir Foundation is the charitable, educational arm of LexNoir, an international network of lawyers connecting the African Diaspora.

This publication, *Franchising in Ethiopia 2014: Legal and Business Considerations*, contains excerpts from *Franchising in Africa 2014: Legal and Business Considerations*. Both works are published by LexNoir Foundation and reflect the points of view of the authors and editors as of the date of publication and do not necessarily represent the opinions, interpretations, or positions of the law firms or organizations with which they are affiliated, nor the opinions, interpretations or positions of LexNoir Foundation or LexNoir.

Nothing contained in this book is to be considered as the rendering of legal advice, either generally or in connection with any specific issues or case. Readers are responsible for obtaining advice from their own legal counsel or other professional. This book, any forms and agreements or other information herein are intended for educational and informational purposes only.

www.lexnoir.org

Table of Contents

Franchising in Ethiopia

Yohannes Assefa and Biset Beyene Molla
Pioneer International Legal Consulting

Bibliography of International Franchise Resources

Kendal H. Tyre, Jr., Diana Vilmenay-Hammond, Pierce Haesung Han, Courtney L. Lindsay, II and Keri McWilliams
Nixon Peabody LLP

Acknowledgment

This book could not have been written without the hard work and dedication of each of the contributing authors and editors. Thank you.

We would like to acknowledge and extend our heartfelt gratitude to Michael Collier and Maria Stallings of the Washington, D.C., office of Nixon Peabody LLP for their invaluable assistance in revising, proofing, and editing this publication.

About the Editors and Authors

Kendal H. Tyre, Jr. – Kendal is a partner in the Washington, D.C., office of Nixon Peabody LLP. He handles domestic and cross-border transactions, including mergers and acquisitions, joint ventures, strategic alliances, licensing, and franchise matters.

In his franchise and licensing practice, Kendal counsels domestic and international franchisors, franchisees, licensors, licensees and distributors regarding U.S. state and federal franchise laws as well as foreign franchise legislation in a variety of jurisdictions. Kendal drafts and provides advice with regard to franchise and license agreements, disclosure documents and area development agreements and has extensive experience drafting and negotiating a variety of other commercial agreements. His client base spans the United States and foreign countries, including South Africa, Kenya, and the United Kingdom.

Kendal is a frequent contributor to franchise publications and a frequent speaker at franchise programs held by the American Bar Association Forum on Franchising and the International Franchise Association.

Kendal is co-chair of the firm's Diversity Action Committee and its Africa group. Kendal is also the executive director of LexNoir Foundation.

E-mail address: ktyre@nixonpeabody.com

Diana Vilmenay-Hammond – Diana is an attorney in the Washington, D.C., office of Nixon Peabody LLP. She is a member of the firm's Franchise & Distribution team.

In her franchise practice, Diana works with domestic and international franchisors on transactional and litigation matters. Specifically, she counsels franchisor clients regarding state and federal franchise laws, disclosure and registration obligations.

Diana drafts and negotiates various commercial agreements, including international franchise and development agreements.

Diana has co-authored numerous articles on franchising and frequently co-hosted the Nixon Peabody franchise law webinar series. Topics have included:

- "Franchise Case Law Round-Up: Implications for Your Franchise," February 15, 2012;
- "Social Media Part II: Best Practices in Protecting Your Brand in the New Media," September 14, 2010; and
- "The Awuah Case: Bellwether or Outlier," May 11, 2010.

Diana received her J.D. from Howard University School of Law and her B.A. from Georgetown University. She is a member of the American Bar Association (Forum on Franchising).

Email address: dvilmenay@nixonpeabody.com

Pierce Haesung Han – Pierce is an associate in Nixon Peabody's Global Business & Transactions group. Pierce focuses his practice on three main areas, assisting clients with a variety of complex business transactions.

- Mergers & Acquisitions: Providing assistance to both public and private clients with various mergers and acquisitions, performing due diligence, drafting and negotiating transaction documents, and facilitating closing and post-closing mechanics.
- International Commercial Transactions: Drafting and negotiating a variety of commercial agreements, including international franchise and development agreements, license agreements, and purchase and sale agreements.
- Federal Securities Law Matters: Assisting public and private clients regarding federal securities laws and stock exchange rules relating to corporate governance and disclosure.

Pierce serves as the Secretary of the Asian Pacific Bar Association Educational Fund (an affiliate of the Asian Pacific American Bar Association of the Greater Washington, D.C., Area).

Pierce received his J.D. from Georgetown University Law Center and his B.A. from Case Western Reserve University. He is admitted to practice in the State of New York and the District of Columbia.

E-mail address: phan@nixonpeabody.com

Courtney L. Lindsay, II – Courtney is an associate in Nixon Peabody's Corporate and Finance practice. In his corporate practice, Courtney assists for-profit and nonprofit entities with transactional matters and corporate governance. In various capacities, Courtney has been involved in multiple merger and acquisition transactions, including drafting and managing due diligence.

Previously, Courtney worked in the legal and business affairs department at a national cable network, where he handled matters related to the network's LLC agreement, including drafting board and member consent agreements.

Courtney received his J.D. from the University of Virginia School of Law and his B.A. from the University of Virginia. He is admitted to practice in the Commonwealth of Virginia and the District of Columbia.

E-mail address: clindsay@nixonpeabody.com

Keri McWilliams – Keri is an associate in the Franchise & Distribution team of Nixon Peabody LLP. Keri works with clients on a number of franchising issues, including obtaining and maintaining franchise registrations in various states, responding to state inquiries regarding trade practices, ongoing compliance with state and federal regulations, and updating franchise disclosure documents. She also handles franchise sales counseling and franchise system issues.

Keri is a member of the American Bar Association's Forum on Franchising, and the Federal and Minnesota State bar associations. She is also a member of Minnesota Women Lawyers and the Minnesota Association of Black Lawyers, and a volunteer in the Volunteer Lawyers Network.

Keri received her J.D. from the Georgetown University Law Center and her B.F.A. from Washington University. She is admitted to practice in the District of Columbia and Minnesota.

E-mail address: kmcwilliams@nixonpeabody.com

Yohannes Assefa – Yohannes is the Managing Director of Pioneer International Legal Consulting in Addis Ababa, Ethiopia. He is an experienced and distinguished business lawyer with business management experience spanning 17 years in the United States and Africa.

Yohannes worked at the Rochester, New York, law firm of Harris Beach PLLC from 2003 to 2007 and then joined the Washington, D.C., office of Hawkins, Delafield and Wood, where he worked as a municipal securities attorney.

In November 2008, Yohannes moved to Ethiopia to help establish the Ethiopia Commodity Exchange (ECX) under a USAID technical advisory contract. Most recently, he served as the Chief of Party of the USAID Ethiopia WTO Accession Plus Project. Currently, he serves as an Adjunct Professor of Law at Addis Ababa University Faculty of Law.

Yohannes earned his law degree in 2001 from Northeastern University School of Law.

E-mail address: abadefar1@gmail.com

Biset Beyene Molla – Biset is an attorney with Pioneer International Legal Consulting in Addis Ababa, Ethiopia. He is an experienced and licensed lawyer with extensive tax and regulatory compliance experience. Biset graduated with an LLB in law from Addis Ababa University, Faculty of Law, in July

2003. Shortly after graduation, he worked for the Ethiopian Federal First Instance Court where he served as an assistant judge until November 2005. He joined Alpha University College as Graduate Assistant II while studying for his master's in Business Law (LLM).

Shortly after he finished his graduate degree, Biset was promoted to the rank of Lecturer at Alpha University College. He later joined the Ethiopian Commodity Exchange as Discipline and Enforcement Manager where he also worked as Assistant General Counselor. In 2010, he was admitted to practice law before the Ethiopian Federal Courts and began practicing law as a litigator. Currently, Biset's practice focuses on litigation before the Ethiopian Federal courts and tax and regulatory consultations. He also advises the National Exchange Actors Association at the Ethiopia Commodity Exchange. Biset also lectures at the Faculty of Law, Addis Ababa University.

E-mail address: bisetbeyene@gmail.com

About the Book

Franchising in Ethiopia 2014: Legal and Business Considerations contains excerpts from the larger work, *Franchising in Africa 2014: Legal and Business Considerations.* Both books serve as practical, succinct, easy-to-use reference tools for lawyers, business people and academics to use in navigating the myriad laws and business issues impacting franchise arrangements on the African continent.

This book provides an overview of the franchise industry in Ethiopia and addresses the typical legal issues confronted when expanding a franchise system in Ethiopia. The larger work, *Franchising in Africa 2014: Legal and Business Considerations,* covers those laws governing franchising in fifteen other African countries—Angola, Botswana, Burundi, Cape Verde, Democratic Republic of Congo, Egypt, Ghana, Kenya, Mozambique, Nigeria, Rwanda, South Africa, Tunisia, Zambia and Zimbabwe.

In both books, an author, who is a legal expert in the designated jurisdiction, addresses the basic questions that a franchise lawyer would need to know to competently represent a client in expanding their franchise system to that country.

Each country chapter organizes a discussion of that country's laws under various headings and in a uniform format. Topics were sent to each country's author in the form of a questionnaire, and each author drafted responses to the questions presented. A general overview relating to the political and economic history of the country at the beginning of each chapter provides an initial context for the regulatory framework.[1]

---

[1] The source of information for these sections is the Central Intelligence Agency, https://www.cia.gov/library/publications/the-world-factbook/ (last visited November 3, 2013).

Apart from an overview of the legal framework for franchising, each book contains other articles and resources that should prove useful to those in the franchise industry.

The authors for each chapter are listed at the beginning of a chapter and their biographical information is listed in the previous section, *About the Editors and Authors*.

Readers should always consult with local counsel in the relevant jurisdiction instead of relying solely on the information contained in this book. The laws governing franchising are evolving and local counsel in Ethiopia are best positioned to provide timely, relevant advice applying the current law to the particular facts of a case.

Franchising in Ethiopia

Yohannes Assefa and Biset Beyene Molla

Pioneer International Legal Consulting

Addis Ababa, Ethiopia

Ethiopia

I.   Introduction

A.   Historical Background of Country

Ethiopia adopted its current constitution in 1994 and the country's first multiparty elections were held in 1995. A border war with Eritrea late in the 1990s ended with a peace treaty in December 2000. In November 2007, the Eritrea-Ethiopia Border Commission (EEBC) issued specific coordinates as virtually demarcating the border and pronounced its work finished. Alleging that the EEBC acted beyond its mandate in issuing the coordinates, Ethiopia has not accepted them and has not withdrawn troops from previously contested areas pronounced by the EEBC as belonging to Eritrea.

B.   Economy of the Country

Ethiopia's economy is based on agriculture, which accounts for 41% of GDP and 85% of total employment. Coffee has been a major export crop. The agricultural sector suffers from poor cultivation practices and frequent drought, but recent joint efforts by the Government of Ethiopia and donors have strengthened Ethiopia's agricultural resilience, contributing to an increased food security and a reduction in the poverty rate of the country . The five-year *Growth and Transformation Plan* that Ethiopia unveiled in October 2010 presents a government-led effort to achieve the country's ambitious development goals. The banking, insurance, and micro-credit industries are restricted to domestic investors, but Ethiopia has attracted significant foreign investment in textiles, leather, commercial agriculture and manufacturing. Under Ethiopia's constitution, the state owns all land and provides long-term leases to the tenants. Land use certificates are now being issued in some areas so that tenants have more recognizable rights to continued occupancy and hence make more concerted efforts to improve their leaseholds. While the economy has grown by an average of 10.6% over the past 10 years, per capita income of $410 per year is among the lowest in the world.

Ethiopia

C.   Franchise Legal Overview

In 2012, the Economist identified Ethiopia as the fastest growing non-oil based economy in Africa, growing by double digits over the past seven years. While Ethiopia's economy is mostly agrarian, the recent expansion of the country's middle class and urban population and its per capita income has made the country ripe for international franchising businesses, especially those involved in the consumer retail business. Yet, few international franchisors have entered the Ethiopian market.

The reasons for the stagnation of the franchising market are many but the most important cause was the 1974 military coup and the subsequent adoption of Soviet-style communist economic policies that wiped out the private sector in Ethiopia. Commercial laws governing businesses and to some degree, franchise arrangements, changed very little during this period and business activity in Ethiopia continued, to a large degree, to be governed by the *Commercial Code of the Empire of Ethiopia*,[2] 1960 (the "Commercial Code"). Consequently, any review of current Ethiopian law governing franchising activity will have to include aspects of both the Commercial Code and new additions and modifications introduced since 1991.

Ethiopia currently does not have per se a body of law specifically governing business franchising. In fact, the term "franchise" or "franchise law" does not appear in the Commercial Code. A review of published legal commentaries on the Commercial Code and contract law also reveals no reference to franchise law. However, there are patchworks of disparate laws that collectively affect the activities of franchisors in Ethiopia.

---

[2]   *Commercial Code of the Empire of Ethiopia, Proclamation No. 166/1960. Federal Negarit Gazeta* Extraordinary Issue, Year, 19, No 3, May 5, 1960.

Ethiopia

II.   Regulatory Requirements

A.   Pre-Sale Disclosure

Please describe any pre-sale franchise disclosure or similar requirements that may apply to franchise transactions.

No pre-sale disclosure or similar requirements apply to any franchise transactions under the laws of Ethiopia.

B.   Governmental Approvals, Registrations, Filing Requirements

Please describe any necessary government approvals, registrations, or filing requirements that may apply to franchise transactions.

Generally, franchise agreements are not required to be registered. They also do not require approval from any governmental or regulatory body under Ethiopian law. Certain aspects of a franchise agreement may, however, be required to be registered at the Ethiopia Investment Agency ("Agency")[3] under legislation regarding technology transfers. Determining what comprises a transfer of technology agreement within the context of a franchise agreement requires a close review of each franchise agreement by local counsel familiar with the regulatory structures of Ethiopian commercial and investment laws.

The Ethiopian Parliament adopted *Investment Reenactment Proclamation 769/2012* (the "2012 Investment Proclamation"). Under this Proclamation, Parliament reaffirmed the Agency's jurisdiction in the registration and regulation of technology transfer agreements[4] and mandated that all technology transfer

---

[3]   The Ethiopian Investment Agency is a government agency established in 1992 to promote private investment, primarily foreign direct investment. The activities of the Agency are supervised by an Investment Board, which is chaired by the Minister of Industry. See http://www.eia.gov.et/english (last visited November 7, 2013).

[4]   *Investment Proclamation No. 769/2012, Federal Nagarit Gazeta*, Year 18,

agreements be submitted to the Agency for "approval and registration."[5]

The 2012 Investment Proclamation refined the definition of "transfer of technology" to mean "the transfer of systemic knowledge for the manufacture of a product, for the application of improvement of a process, or for the rendering of a service, including management and marketing technologies."[6] The definition does not extend to transactions involving the mere sale or lease of goods.[7] Franchise agreements may fall under the purview of the Investment Proclamations if a franchise agreement includes, for example, a marketing technology, and proprietary business processes, and/or specified machines that could be used for the production of goods or for rendition of a service. In these instances, the franchise agreement may require registration with the Agency.

See also Section V (Trademarks) of this chapter relating to the registration of licenses with the Ethiopian Intellectual Property Office and Section III (Currency) of this chapter relating to potential requirements for the remittance of foreign currency.

C. Limits of Fees and Typical Term of Franchise Agreement

Please describe any limits upon the nature and extent of fees and the term of a typical franchise agreement.

No. 63, September 17, 2012, Article 21. This Article reiterated what was provided in *Proclamation No. 280/2002 Article 18* (renumbered Article 20, Amendment Proclamation 375/2003), without, however, affecting the jurisdiction of the Ethiopian Investment Agency with regard to registration and approval of transfers of technology.

[5]   *Id.*

[6]   *Id.*; Article 2 (10).

[7]   *Id.*

Ethiopia

1.   Limits on Nature of Fees

For the most part, the 2012 Investment Proclamation replaced an earlier regulatory regime. However, it is unclear what aspects of the repealed regulations remain in effect and applicable to transfer of technology agreements. For those franchise agreements deemed to be technology transfers, the repealed regulations regulated fees and payments. While payments could be made on the basis of lump-sum, royalties, or a combination of the two,[8] the procedure and currency of payment as well as the price indexation could be freely determined by the parties to the agreement.[9] However, the repealed regulations prohibited any fixed minimum royalty payments to the supplier of technology. If provisions of accessories, components, and spare parts were to be made available by the supplier of technology, the agreement had to provide that the prices of these articles should not be higher than the current international prices. It is unclear on what basis and standards the Agency will justify an approval or denial of certain aspects of transfer of technology agreements but the repealed regulations may provide some insight.

III.   Currency

If all payments under a franchise agreement must be made in immediately available U.S. Dollars, please advise as to any restrictions, reporting requirements, or regulations concerning the exchange, repatriation, or remittance of U.S. Dollars.

There is no legal restriction on the payment of money in foreign currency to a franchisor that, under a franchise agreement, provides technology, proprietary business process or other vital business services to a local franchisee. While the details are left to the National Bank of Ethiopia ("NBE"), the free transfer of funds in foreign currency has been clearly reaffirmed in the 2012 Investment Proclamation.

---

[8]   *Transfer of Technology Council of Ministers Regulation No. 121/93* ("TOT Regulation") 20 (2).

[9]   *Id.*

Ethiopia

The *National Bank Directives* provide for remittance of foreign currency by a resident business to foreign suppliers of technology and other services necessary for conducting of their business.[10] A franchisee that has evidence of debt due to a franchisor under the franchise agreement normally has the right to obtain foreign currency to effect payments to the franchisor.

Once a foreign investor is recognized by the NBE, an application may be made for remittance. To do so, one is required to provide evidence of payment of the business tax (under the *Income Tax Proclamation*). If the foreign investor is a business organization, the applicant must show evidence of payment of taxes on dividends from the tax authority as well as minutes of the meetings of partners or shareholders, as the case may be, showing the amount of profit declared as a dividend by the shareholders or partners.

The foreign investor or an agent must then file the application for grant of remittance through a commercial bank in which he or she holds a savings account in foreign or local currencies. Given the scarcity of hard currency available to the nation's foreign trade, it is always subject to prioritization. The franchisee may not have hard currency to readily pay its foreign franchisor.

There are areas designated by regulations as priority areas through which the government gives investors incentives including making available foreign currency for financing any debt they may contract including royalties, etc. If the area of investment is one the government considers by law a priority area for investment because of its potential to attract tourism, job opportunities, or increase foreign currency earnings in return, it may be easy to obtain the permission of NBE for the required hard currency.

---

[10] *The National .Foreign Exchange Regulation Directives* provide the details of how remittances may be made. As far as transfer of technology is concerned, the Investment Agency registered certificate is one requirement for remittance.

Ethiopia

In case the franchisor is not a partner in the business of the franchisee but entitled only to a royalty under the franchise agreement, the NBE will require the franchisee to present the franchise agreement under which the royalty is due to the franchisor. It is important to exercise caution in drafting franchise agreements to avoid any risk of rejection on the basis of exorbitant prices.

IV. Taxes, Tariffs, and Duties

Please do not provide any in-depth comments on tax structuring. However, please provide your general comments on the typical amount of withholding tax that would apply and whether a "gross-up" provision contained in a franchise agreement would be enforceable in your country.

The *Income Tax Proclamation* provides for withholding of taxes on royalties payable to nonresident licensors[11] and on dividends.[12] The legislation calls for a 5% withholding for royalties and a 10% withholding for dividends.[13] It is also important to note the *Value Added Tax ("VAT") Proclamation No. 286/2002.* Under this proclamation, a VAT registered person who receives service from a nonresident person and has to pay for such service is bound to withhold a 15% VAT from the amount payable, unless the transaction is exempted[14] from payment of VAT under

---

[11] Income Tax Proclamation No. 286/2002; Federal Negarit Gazeta, Year 8, No. 34 4th July 2002; Article 31/3.

[12] *Id.*; Article 34/1.

[13] Ethiopia has agreements on avoidance of double taxation with the Czech Republic, France, Tunisia, Algeria, Israel, Turkey, South Africa, Yemen, Russia, Kuwait, Italy and Romania.

[14] Exemptions under Article 8 (2) include (a) the sale or transfer of a used dwelling, or the lease of a dwelling; (b) the rendering of financial services; (c) the supply or import of national or foreign currency (except for that used for numismatic purposes), and securities; (d) the import of gold to be transferred to the National Bank of Ethiopia; (e) the rendering by religious organizations of religious or church related services; (f) the import or supply of prescription drugs specified in directives issued by the Minister of Health, and the rendering of medical services; (g) the rendering of educational services provided by educational institutions, as well as child

Ethiopia

Article 8 of the Proclamation.[15] This is irrespective of whether the customer receiving the services from the nonresident is registered for VAT or not.

There is nothing stated, expressed, or implied, in Ethiopian tax law prohibiting provisions related to gross-ups. Therefore, the general view among tax authorities is that the amount of withholding tax grossed-up may be, in the worst case scenario, considered earnings by the non-resident/recipient and earnings on which the same rate of tax applies.

V.   Trademarks

Please advise us as to whether there are any special requirements for granting a valid trademark license, including the use of a registered user agreement or a short trademark license agreement and any required filing of such an agreement with the trademark authorities.

Under Ethiopian law, a right relating to a registered trademark may be assigned or licensed in whole or in part. The Trademark

---

care services for children at pre-school institutions; (h) the supply of goods and rendering of services in the form of humanitarian aid, as well as import of goods transferred to state agencies of Ethiopia and public organizations for the purpose of rehabilitation after natural disasters, industrial accidents, and catastrophes; (i) the supply of electricity, kerosene, and water; (j) goods imported by the government, organizations, institutions or projects exempted from duties and other import taxes to the extent provided by law or by agreement; (k) supplies by the post office authorized under the Ethiopian Postal Services Proclamation, other than services rendered for a fee or commission; (l) the provision of transport; (m) permits and license fees; (n) the import of goods to the extent provided under Schedule 2 of the Customs Tariffs Regulations; (o) the supply of goods or services by a workshop employing disabled individuals if more than 60 percent of the employees are disabled; and (p) the import or supply of books and other printed materials to the extent provided in regulations. The Ministry of Finance and Economic Development has been authorized to exempt, by directives, other goods and services not listed under Article 8 of the Proclamation.

[15] *Value Added Tax Proclamation No. 285/2002, Article 23/1, Federal Negarit Gazeta*, Year 8, No 33, July 4, 2002.

Ethiopia

Registration and Protection Proclamation No. 501/2006 ("Trademark Proclamation") provides that a license contract must be made in writing and submitted to the Ethiopian Intellectual Property Office ("EIPO") for registration. Subsequent modifications or cancellations are also subject to registration with EIPO.[16] The contract should indicate whether the license extends to all or part of the goods or services for which the trademark is registered.[17] If it does not contain any references to the scope of the license, the effect is that the licensee is free to use it for all products for which the trademark is registered. The license contract will have no effect on third parties until it is registered by EIPO and publicized by a designated intellectual property gazette (which does not exist to date) or a paper with nationwide circulation, such as the state-owned, Amharic daily paper, *Addis Zemen* and the English daily *Ethiopian Herald*. In its publication of the license contract for a public announcement, EIPO is bound to keep the details confidential.[18]

The trademark owner may grant a license for the use of the trademark by the franchisee within a limited territory or with respect to limited products that the trademark normally covers in its registration.[19]

A long awaited implementing directive of the Trademark Proclamation became effective February 2013. The EIPO

---

[16] *Trademark Registration and Protection Proclamation No. 501/2006, Federal Negarit Gazeta*, Year 12, No. 37, July 7, 2006. Article 29/2.

[17] *Id.* Article 29/1.

[18] *Id.* Article 29/2.

[19] *Id.* Article 31/2/a. Though the practice has yet to evolve, any limitation concerning the territory in which the trademark may be used by the franchisee/licensee may constitute market segmentation for the purpose of the *Trade Practice and Consumer Protection Proclamation No. 685/2010.* This issue has yet to be decided. In the opinion of these authors, as *Article 13/1/a/iii of the Trade Practice and Consumer Protection Proclamation* states in general terms that "agreements as to market or consumer segmentation" are deemed to be anticompetitive, segmentation of the market by territory based on trademarks is acceptable because the trademark law should prevail over a law that is general in character.

regulation and the directive deal with a number of trademark law issues and requirements, but there are still some concerns for franchisors and other businesses, even those that have previously registered marks.[20] For example, marks registered in Ethiopia prior to enactment of the Trademark Proclamation, as well as certain marks registered under the Trademark Proclamation, must be re-registered, even if the current term of validity of the marks has not expired.[21] In sum, a new application must be filed with the EIPO and the filer must adhere to the registration requirements in the directive and implementing regulation. Marks registered after the Trademark Proclamation became effective must be amended so that their registration certificates reflect a new term of validity.[22]

Despite positive changes to the law as a result of the directive, some potentially burdensome filing requirements remain.[23] For example, a foreign trademark application must be filed together with an authenticated power of attorney.[24] Moreover, a foreign trademark application must be accompanied by a copy of the home registration certificate—a certificate issued in any country outside of Ethiopia—or a copy of a certificate of business license.[25]

VI.　Restrictions on Transfer

Please advise as to whether there are any restrictions (1) on a franchisor to restrict transfers by a master franchisee, any interest in a master franchisee, or the assets of the master franchisee or (2) the ability of a master franchisee to control

---

[20] Kendal H. Tyre, Jr., Yohannes Assefa, & Getachew Mengistie *New Intellectual Property Regulation Requires Scramble to Protect Marks in Ethiopia*, NIXON PEABODY LLP: FRANCHISE LAW ALERT (October 2013).

[21] *Id.*

[22] *Id.*

[23] *Id.*

[24] *Id.*

[25] *Id.*

and/or restrict transfers of a subfranchisee's rights under a master franchise agreement, interest in the subfranchisee, or the assets of the subfranchisee.

Any restrictions on the franchisor, vis à vis its interests and assets in the master franchisee (or the master franchisee vis à vis its interests and assets in the subfranchisee), depends on the terms of the contract. However, Article 201 of the Commercial Code provides a clear restriction on any assignment without the written consent of the lessor, which, in this case, is the franchisor. The law restricts the lessee because, under the law, "a contract of lease is made on the basis of the personal qualification of the lessee." Franchisor relies on the personal and/or organizational qualification of the franchisee when determining whether the franchisee will maintain the goodwill and standards of the business. Accordingly, assigning or sub-franchising the franchise without the prior consent of the franchisor (or the master franchisee, as applicable) is prohibited.

VII. Termination

Please advise us as to any laws relating to termination in your country, such as agency laws, required indemnity provisions, notice or "good cause" requirements, or other laws affecting termination of a franchise agreement. Please describe.

The law of contracts stipulates that contracting parties, and only they, may determine the contents of their contract, subject to the mandatory provisions of the law.[26] A franchise agreement is no different. As long as there is no specific law to which it has to be subjected, the parties are free to determine the terms of the contract and advance their interests.

---

[26] Article 1731/2.

Ethiopia

VIII. Governing Law, Jurisdiction, and Dispute Resolution

A.   Choice of Law of Foreign Jurisdiction

Please confirm whether the choice of law of a foreign jurisdiction would likely to be upheld under the law of the country, except for certain matters such as trademarks, bankruptcy, and competition matters, which we assume would be governed by the law in your country.

Recent draft legislation for consideration by the Federal House of People's Representatives provides contractual parties may, in the absence of specific law to the contrary, stipulate in advance to choice of law provisions.[27] The parties, however, must choose from among a list of choices expressly provided in the draft rules which are:

> *"...the law of nationality, the law of domicile, the law of the place where the transaction was made, the law of the place where the subject matter is situated, the law of the place where the transaction is to be performed, or the law of the place which is reasonably connected to the matter."*[28]

As it now stands, the parties may not opt for any other law that cannot be identified as one of the above. Thus, assuming the draft legislation passes, franchising parties may agree on any one of the available choices to govern the substance of the franchise agreement in the event of a dispute. However, the choice of law must be explicit or clearly evident from the agreement or from the circumstances of the case.[29]

---

[27]   *Draft Proclamation to Provide for Federal Rules of Private International Law*, Article 21/1.

[28]   *Id.*

[29]   *Id.* Article 72/3

Ethiopia

Please note that currently the 2012 Investment Proclamation provides that transfer of technology agreements are subject to Ethiopian law except where the parties agree to settle their disputes through negotiation, conciliation, or arbitration. Although untested in practice, there are no restrictions on choice of law clauses as long as the choice has no objective of bypassing the application of laws with important public policy bearings.

B. International Arbitration Dispute Resolution

Please confirm that a court in your country would honor an election of international arbitration dispute resolution, and therefore refuse to hear any disputes arising under a franchise agreement.

The *Civil Code* (Articles 3307 to 3346) and the *Civil Procedure Code* (Article 244/2/g, Articles 274 to 277 and 315 through 319) recognize out of court settlement of disputes be it by arbitration, conciliation, or mediation. Contracting parties who have a dispute settlement provision in their contract or those who agree later to arbitrate or conciliate are bound by the terms of their agreement and must submit any dispute to these mechanisms for resolution. Most international transactions with Ethiopian parties provide for international arbitration. The courts uphold such provisions and have procedures for their enforcement in the *Civil Procedure Code of the Empire of Ethiopia, 1965.*[30]

Ethiopia is not a signatory to the *Convention on the Recognition and Enforcement of Foreign Arbitral Awards* (the "New York Convention").

IX. Non-Competition Provisions

If the franchise agreement prohibits the master franchisee from engaging in certain competitive activities during the term of the

---

[30] *Civil Procedure Code Decree No. 52/1965. Negarit Gazeta*, Extraordinary Issue, Year, 25, No. 3. Article 461.

Ethiopia

agreement, and for a 12-month period after the termination or expiration of the agreement, please comment on the enforceability of non-competition covenants in your country.

Non-competition provisions are well-known to Ethiopian law. Under the Commercial Code, the seller of a business has to refrain, for a duration of five years from the time of sale, from any act of competition that is likely to injure the buyer.[31] The seller may not carry on a trade similar to the one he sold in the vicinity where the sold business is operated by the buyer. Furthermore, the contract of sale may provide the extent of the prohibition and fix the duration in which the non-competition restriction should last, which, in any case, cannot be for more than five years. It is also stipulated under Article 55 of the Commercial Code that a commercial agent may be bound by the contract of agency not to carry on a private trade similar to that of the principal upon the termination of the agreement. Contractual restrictions on the agent, however, may not be effective for more than five years notwithstanding any provision to the contrary.[32] Given these legal standards currently recognized by Ethiopian law, it is reasonable to conclude that reasonable non-competition provisions in a franchise agreement will be enforceable.

X.   Language Requirements

Does the law in your country require that a franchise agreement be translated into the local language in order to be enforceable between the parties?

There is no requirement that franchise agreements be translated into the local language to be enforceable. English is acceptable. Generally, however, if the franchise agreement is disputed in court, the party introducing the franchise agreement as evidence is required to provide an official translation of the document in the official working language of the court. Federal courts require

---

[31]   Article 158.

[32]   Article 55/2.

14

Ethiopia

translation to Amharic while state courts require translation to their respective working languages.

XI. Other Significant Matters

Please advise as to whether there are any significant matters not addressed above of which a franchisor should be aware in connection with its entering into a franchise agreement in your country.

The *Commercial Registration and Business Licensing Proclamation*[33] issued in June 2010 by the Federal legislative body has provided strict requirements for applicants to produce a valid certificate of professional competence issued by the relevant sectoral public body for an effective business license to be issued by the Ministry of Trade or the relevant regional bureau. Thus, a franchisee who may want to commence business under a license granted by a franchise agreement will likely need to seek approval of the public body in charge of issuing certificates of competence for the business in question.

---

[33] *Proclamation to Provide for Commercial Registration and Business Licensing* No. 686/2010. *Federal Negarit Gazeta* 16th, Year No. 42. 24th July 2010, Article 32/8.

Bibliography of International Franchise Resources

Kendal H. Tyre, Jr., Diana Vilmenay-Hammond, Pierce Haesung Han, Courtney L. Lindsay, II and Keri McWilliams

Nixon Peabody LLP

Washington, D.C.

I.   General International Resources

Mark Abell, Gary R. Duvall, and Andrea Oricchio Kirsh, *International Franchise Legislation* B1, ABA FORUM ON FRANCHISING (1996)

Kathleen C. Anderson and Anthony M. Stiegler, *Put Muscle in Your Marks: Enforcing Intellectual Property Rights* W14, ABA FORUM ON FRANCHISING (1995)

Richard M. Asbill and Jane W. LaFranchi, *International Franchise Sales Laws—A Survey* W7, ABA FORUM ON FRANCHISING (2005)

Jeffery A. Brimer, Alison C. McElroy, and John Pratt, *Going International: What Additional Restraints Will You Face?* W4, ABA FORUM ON FRANCHISING (2011)

Michael G. Brennan, Alexander Konigsberg, and Philip F. Zeidman, *Globetrotting: A Workshop on International Franchising* 10/W8, ABA FORUM ON FRANCHISING (1994)

Michael G. Brennan, Alexander Konigsberg, and Philip F. Zeidman, *Globetrotting: Strategies for Launching U.S. Franchisors Abroad* 2/P2, ABA FORUM ON FRANCHISING (1994)

Christopher P. Bussert and Jennifer Dolman, *Regaining Your Trademark After Abandonment or Misappropriation* W7, ABA FORUM ON FRANCHISING (2011)

Ronald T. Coleman and Linda K. Stevens, *Trade Secrets and Confidential Information: Rights and Remedies* W2, ABA FORUM ON FRANCHISING (2000)

Finola Cunningham, *Commerce Department Helps Franchisors Go Global*, in FRANCHISING WORLD 63 (Dec. 2005)

Michael R. Daigle and Alex S. Konigsberg, *Meeting Off-Shore Disclosure and Contract Requirements* F/W13, ABA FORUM ON FRANCHISING (1992)

Jennifer Dolman, Robert A. Lauer, and Lawrence M. Weinberg, *Structuring International Master Franchise Relationships for Success and Responding When Things Go Awry* W22, ABA FORUM ON FRANCHISING (2007)

Gary R. Duvall, Paul Jones, and Jane LaFranchi, *Planning for the International Enforcement of Franchise Agreements* W6, ABA FORUM ON FRANCHISING (1999)

William Edwards, *International Expansion: Do Opportunities Outweigh Challenges?* in FRANCHISING WORLD (February 2008)

George J. Eydt and Stuart Hershman, *Bringing a Foreign Franchise System to the United States* W9, ABA FORUM ON FRANCHISING (2009)

William A. Finkelstein and Louis T. Pirkey, *International Trademarks* W15, ABA FORUM ON FRANCHISING (1991)

William A. Finkelstein, *Protecting Trademarks Internationally: Current Strategies and Developments* B3, ABA FORUM ON FRANCHISING (1996)

Stephen Giles, Lou H. Jones, and Lawrence Weinberg, *Negotiating and Documenting Complex International Franchise Agreements* W21, ABA FORUM ON FRANCHISING (2006)

Steven M. Goldman, Stephen Giles, Marc Israel, and Stanley Wong, *Competition Round Up from Around the World* LB2, ABA FORUM ON FRANCHISING (2004)

David C. Gryce and E. Lynn Perry, *Trademarks and Copyrights in the International Arena* 6/W4, ABA FORUM ON FRANCHISING (1993)

Kenneth S. Kaplan, Andrew P. Loewinger, and Penelope J. Ward, *System Standards in International Franchising* W14, ABA FORUM ON FRANCHISING (2005)

Edward Levitt and Jorge Mondragon, *A Survey of International Legal Traps and How to Avoid Them—Beyond the Franchise Laws* W20, ABA FORUM ON FRANCHISING (2007)

Ned Levitt, Kendal H. Tyre, and Penny Ward, *The Impossible Dream: Controlling Your International Franchise System* W4, ABA FORUM ON FRANCHISING (2010)

Michael K. Lindsey and Andrew P. Loewinger, *International (Non-U.S.) Franchise Disclosure Requirements* W9, ABA FORUM ON FRANCHISING (2002)

Andrew P. Loewinger and John Pratt, *Recent Changes and Trends in International Franchise Laws* W4, ABA FORUM ON FRANCHISING (2008)

Andrew P. Loewinger and Thomas M. Pitegoff, *Avoiding the Long Arm of the Law in International Franchising: Issues and Approaches* W8, ABA FORUM ON FRANCHISING (1995)

Craig J. Madson and Katherine C. Spelman, *Similarity and Confusion in the Intellectual Property Arena* W11, ABA FORUM ON FRANCHISING (1997)

Christopher A. Nowak, John Pratt, and Carl E. Zwisler, *Franchising Internationally with Countries with Opaque Legal Systems* W20, ABA FORUM ON FRANCHISING (2006)

E. Lynn Perry and John L. Sullivan Jr., *Trademark Compliance and Enforcement Techniques* E/W12, ABA FORUM ON FRANCHISING (1992)

Marcel Portmann, *Franchising Sector Proves Global Reach*, in FRANCHISING WORLD (January 2007)

John Pratt and Luiz Henrique O. do Amaral, *Civil Law for Common Law Practitioners (or How to Draft an Agreement for Use Overseas)* W4, ABA FORUM ON FRANCHISING (2002)

Kirk W. Reilly, Robert F. Salkowski and Geoffrey B. Shaw, *Determining the Rules of Engagement in Litigation Here and Abroad* W5, ABA FORUM ON FRANCHISING (2008)

Catherine Riesterer and Frank Zaid, *Basics of International Franchising* L/B2, ABA FORUM ON FRANCHISING (1997)

W. Andrew Scott and Christopher N. Wormald, *Stranger in a Strange Land: Contrasting Franchising in International Expansion* W2, ABA FORUM ON FRANCHISING (2003)

Donald Smith and Erik Wulff, *International Franchising: The Unraveling of an International Franchise Relationship* 15/W13, ABA FORUM ON FRANCHISING (1993)

Frank Zaid, Pamela Mills, and Michael Santa Maria, *Essential Issues in International Franchising* LB/1, ABA FORUM ON FRANCHISING (2001)

II.   African Resources

Joyce G. Mazero and J. Perry Maisonneuve, *Franchising in the Middle East and North Africa* W2, ABA FORUM ON FRANCHISING (2009)

Kendal H. Tyre, Jr. and Diana Vilmenay-Hammond, *Franchise World: A Burgeoning Middle Class Spurs Franchise Investment in Africa*, MINORITY BUSINESS ENTREPRENEUR (November 2012)

Kendal H. Tyre, Jr., *IP Protection May Promote Additional Franchise Growth in Africa*, NIXON PEABODY LLP: FRANCHISING BUSINESS & LAW ALERT (September 2012)

Kendal H. Tyre, Jr., *Market Potential for Franchising in Africa*, NIXON PEABODY LLP: FRANCHISING BUSINESS & LAW ALERT (June 2011)

Kendal H. Tyre, Jr. and Courtney L. Lindsay, II, *Continued Growth of Franchising in Africa*, NIXON PEABODY LLP: FRANCHISE LAW ALERT (April 2013)

Kendal H. Tyre, Jr. and Courtney L. Lindsay, II, *Pan African Franchise Federation Holds Inaugural Meeting*, NIXON PEABODY LLP: AFRICA ALERT (June 2013)

Kendal H. Tyre, Jr. and Courtney L. Lindsay, II, *White House Encouraging Private Investment and Transparency in Sub-Saharan Africa*, NIXON PEABODY LLP: AFRICA ALERT (August 2012)

Kendal H. Tyre, Jr. and Diana Vilmenay-Hammond, *African Economic Growth Impacts Franchising on the Continent*, NIXON PEABODY LLP: FRANCHISE LAW ALERT (July 2012)

Kendal H. Tyre, Jr. and Diana Vilmenay-Hammond, *Franchising in Africa*, in FRANCHISING WORLD (August 2013)

John Sotos and Sam Hall, *African Franchising: Cross-Continent Momentum*, in FRANCHISING WORLD (June 2007)

A.   Angola

João Afonso Fialho, *Franchising in Angola*, in FRANCHISING IN AFRICA: LEGAL AND BUSINESS CONSIDERATIONS 91-105 (Kendal H. Tyre, Jr. & Diana Vilmenay-Hammond eds. 2012)

B. Botswana

Bonzo Makgalemele, *Franchising in Botswana*, in FRANCHISING IN AFRICA: LEGAL AND BUSINESS CONSIDERATIONS 107-117 (Kendal H. Tyre, Jr. & Diana Vilmenay-Hammond eds. 2012)

C. Cape Verde

João Afonso Fialho, *Franchising in Cape Verde*, in FRANCHISING IN AFRICA: LEGAL AND BUSINESS CONSIDERATIONS 119-132 (Kendal H. Tyre, Jr. & Diana Vilmenay-Hammond eds. 2012)

D. Egypt

Girgis Abd El-Shahid, *Franchising in Eqypt*, in FRANCHISING IN AFRICA: LEGAL AND BUSINESS CONSIDERATIONS 133-142 (Kendal H. Tyre, Jr. & Diana Vilmenay-Hammond eds. 2012)

A. Safaa El Din El Oteifi, *Egypt*, in INTERNATIONAL FRANCHISING EGY/1 (Dennis Campbell gen. ed. 2011)

E. Ethiopia

Yohannes Assefa and Biset Beyene Molla, *Franchising in Ethiopia*, in FRANCHISING IN AFRICA: LEGAL AND BUSINESS CONSIDERATIONS 143-157 (Kendal H. Tyre, Jr. & Diana Vilmenay-Hammond eds. 2012)

Kendal H. Tyre, Jr., Yohannes Assefa and Getachew Mengistie Alemu, *New Intellectual Property Regulation Requires Scramble to Protect Marks in Ethiopia*, NIXON PEABODY LLP: AFRICA ALERT (October 2013)

F. Ghana

Divine K.D. Letsa and Hawa Tejansie Ajei, *Franchising in Ghana*, in FRANCHISING IN AFRICA: LEGAL AND BUSINESS CONSIDERATIONS 159-167 (Kendal H. Tyre, Jr. & Diana Vilmenay-Hammond eds. 2012)

G.   Libya

Kendal H. Tyre, Jr. & Diana Vilmenay-Hammond, *First U.S. Franchise Opens in Libya*, NIXON PEABODY LLP: AFRICA ALERT (August 2012)

H.   Mozambique

Diogo Xavier da Cunha, *Franchising in Mozambique*, in FRANCHISING IN AFRICA: LEGAL AND BUSINESS CONSIDERATIONS 169-182 (Kendal H. Tyre, Jr. & Diana Vilmenay-Hammond eds. 2012)

I.   Nigeria

Theo Emuwa and Bimbola Fowler-Ekar, *Franchising in Nigeria*, in FRANCHISING IN AFRICA: LEGAL AND BUSINESS CONSIDERATIONS 183-198 (Kendal H. Tyre, Jr. & Diana Vilmenay-Hammond eds. 2012)

Kendal H. Tyre, Jr. and Theo Emuwa, *Nigerian Franchising: Making Your Way Through the Thicket*, NIXON PEABODY LLP: FRANCHISE LAW ALERT (June 2005)

J.   South Africa

Eugene Honey, *Franchising and the New Consumer Protection Bill*, BOWMAN GILFILLAN (March 2008)

Eugene Honey, *Franchising and the Consumer Protection Bill*, BOWMAN GILFILLAN (May 2008)

Eugene Honey, *Pitfalls and Difficulties with the CPA*, ADAMS & ADAMS (March 2013)

Eugene Honey, *Disclosure is Compulsory*, ADAMS & ADAMS (May 2013)

Eugene Honey and Wim Alberts, *Fundamental Consumer Rights: The Right to Equality*, BOWMAN GILFILLAN (March 2009)

Eugene Honey and Wim Alberts, *The Reach of the Consumer Protection Bill: The Final*, BOWMAN GILFILLAN (March 2009)

Eugene Honey, *South Africa*, in GETTING THE DEAL THROUGH: FRANCHISE (2013) 172-178 (Philip F. Zeidman ed. 2013)

Taswell Papier, *Franchising in South Africa*, in FRANCHISING IN AFRICA: LEGAL AND BUSINESS CONSIDERATIONS 199-224 (Kendal H. Tyre, Jr. & Diana Vilmenay-Hammond eds. 2012)

Kendal H. Tyre, Jr., *A New Legal Landscape for Franchising in South Africa*, NIXON PEABODY LLP: FRANCHISING BUSINESS & LAW ALERT (September 2009)

K.   Tunisia

Yessine Ferah, *Franchising in Tunisia*, in FRANCHISING IN AFRICA: LEGAL AND BUSINESS CONSIDERATIONS 225-245 (Kendal H. Tyre, Jr. & Diana Vilmenay-Hammond eds. 2012)

Kendal H. Tyre, Jr., Diana Vilmenay-Hammond, and Yessine Ferah, *New Franchise Legislation in Tunisia*, NIXON PEABODY LLP: FRANCHISE LAW ALERT (September 2010)

L.   Zambia

Mabvuto Sakala, *Franchising in Zambia*, in FRANCHISING IN AFRICA: LEGAL AND BUSINESS CONSIDERATIONS 247-255 (Kendal H. Tyre, Jr. & Diana Vilmenay-Hammond eds. 2012)